AF437410

RECKLESS *at* 2AM

of love, loss and longing

Copyright © Esvee Menon
All Rights Reserved.

ISBN 979-8-88606-726-2

This book has been published with all efforts taken to make the material error-free after the consent of the author. However, the author and the publisher do not assume and hereby disclaim any liability to any party for any loss, damage, or disruption caused by errors or omissions, whether such errors or omissions result from negligence, accident, or any other cause.

While every effort has been made to avoid any mistake or omission, this publication is being sold on the condition and understanding that neither the author nor the publishers or printers would be liable in any manner to any person by reason of any mistake or omission in this publication or for any action taken or omitted to be taken or advice rendered or accepted on the basis of this work. For any defect in printing or binding the publishers will be liable only to replace the defective copy by another copy of this work then available.

Kings fell in forty nights. Hearts broke and mended themselves back again.
The tectonic plates underneath me moved an inch
and in forty days, a faith found its God resurrected.

The world could have turned topsy turvy in forty ways.
But for forty days, forty pages and forty phrases,
Some stayed.

thank you

Yuvraj Juneja

Deepak Virmani   Urvi Ganatra

Kalpak Bhinde   Mansi Majithia

Book designed by Ruddhi Merchant & Sneha Nair

contents

in defence of the reckless

Words are those disorderly things you find floating in the air.

You then pick and place them at your will, and then call it poetry. Or so I thought.

My first attempt to stitch a thought with rhyme was for a juvenile email signature. They began as a couplet, that revamped itself as a short prose, then turned reckless by mutating into any form it feels like. It was quite audacious that way. Unpredictable. Inconsiderate. Yet, it loved to be written.

A lost memory? Jot it down. A fragile friendship? Frantic scribbling. A secret affair? A perfect sauce. It was like therapy. Scratch that. It was therapy. I expressed everything in utter confidence and with zero consequences.

And so, it continued until year 2020, when the world paused.

The lockdown hit, and a challenge on social media seemed like an excellent distraction. But who knew what was to come?

It was a paradox. A part of us refused to fathom the tenacity of the situation, but it also struggled with feeble impermanence of everything precious and rare. Time was being a bitch.

But for forty nights, I picked one feeling and painted the walls of my world with it. Numbness, fright, loss, pain, euphoria, stability, tranquillity – all had their days during this lockdown. They translated themselves on to the pages in their own way. The words, too, marched to their beats.

But not all.

Some lay hidden between the lines, still hanging in the air…

Waiting to be read, waiting to be tamed.

u & i

It was there, where,

a stitch and a tear

was busy reaching through a crack,

to a spot of mess and stolen smiles.

Side profiles,

Black and white lines and

two blank spaces,

which stood by

to fill itself with the tales of

You and I.

a longing in these times

Do you close your eyes when you hug me?

Do you look for my fingers between yours?

Do you smile a little when you catch me staring?

Or worry when you don't see my name on your screen?

Do you think we mistook those moments for a dream?

Because it flashed and then disappeared as it did.

Do you think we said all those words on a whim?

Because they carried three truckloads of feelings within.

Do you think day-dreaming would do the trick?

Or would our insides ache to sense each other's air?

But if you knew, our time together ended this quick,

Would you have hugged me tighter?

Would you have really dared?

because

You won't hold me close; you won't let me feel the most,

Of your need, and that feeling your eyes boast.

You won't let me go, won't let others give what you don't.

Yet avoiding my doubts that rose, I choose our silent moments of gold.

For what we have is right, no matter what they feel like.

Even knowing that someday I will walk it past, leaving you at last,

then turn to see you change, emote and embrace,

the many ways I wanted you to profess, to care, to reveal your melting gaze.

Yet in the corner

of your eyes, I know I shall stay,

Near the path where those tears run astray.

At ease then you will sneak a look,

to see if I am alright, still smiling, still true...

To that heart you once touched,

cradled and cared with your silence.

And I shall hold your absent hand through,

to love someone because I once loved you.

all it takes

Those dramas on the screen,

will one day talk about you.

How you found ways to silently scream,

while the world healed from a bad bout of flu.

How you learnt the magic of second looks,

the odd charm of dusty books,

old conversations renewed,

curious details, buried outlooks,

long eye contacts, hidden words, hidden moods.

And while you indulged in the crisp air and leaves that curled,

atop a building, a little bird fluttered in her nook,

and sang a sonnet on. To save the entire world,

a crew of rogue microbes is all it took.

And that moment shall come,

when life becomes,

even better than midnight dreams.

Call me wrong, call me foolish,

to follow a silent scream.

But once time had brought, a blue sky forth.

Now I want it here, right from my thoughts.

And gazing at the coral sky turning grey,

I'll wait here awake, awake for a dandier day.

this sunday

Sleeping in late, didn't feel that special, did it?
What about those neverending noons?
Cuddling on the bed seemed oddly ordinary,
long best friend calls, not so cool.

Now that this doesn't feel like an old-school Sunday,
do you wonder, what else we took for granted,
that could end with no warning, way too soon?

fireball

The embers of your past,

glow intense, glow bright.

The joker with his pride,

is unaware of the sparks you hide.

One word is all it takes,

for it to burn through your eyes.

You first let a flame escape,

to then unleash a wildfire outside.

finding a friend

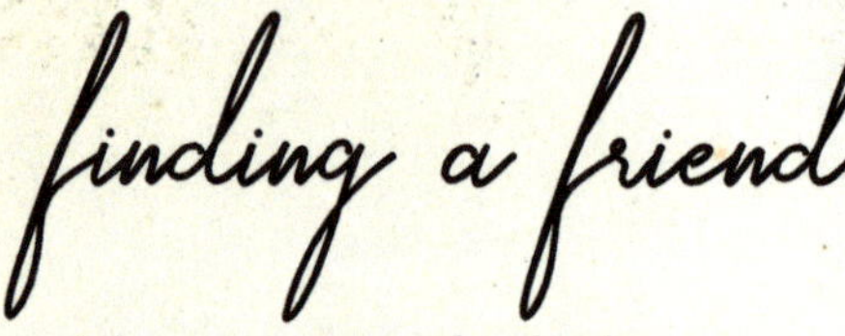

Mornings were not kind to her.

They felt like a vortex of a looming tragedy or a numbing ache.

She couldn't explain it to the world.

Then there was this figure, in grey and black with

a large beak and demanding eyes.

Was it a him or a her?

She shared with him some stale bread and embarrassing secrets.

Two weeks later, he brought a half-eaten piece of a rodent's head.

It was a gift.

A rare appreciation in her life after a long time.

The numbing ache remained.

But the daily 15 seconds provided

her with some breathing space.

The silent, hungry crow was

now her only friend.

Slowly, her mornings were making

a little more sense.

just a word

A smile has a voice.
It is low and it is mild.
Like the word you just
whispered to me,
A word that made my day,
A sweet little poetry.

amma

That singular figure was everywhere.

At her workplace, miles away,

or toiling in the kitchen,

or dropping me to school,

at each school function,

each festival, each family occasion.

Every vacation.

Omnipresent.

Sometimes miserable,

but always there.

So, when the nightmares of the

'Teen-mundi-wali' struck,

at midnight I snuck into her bed.

It was no wonder that I was convinced,

she had a superhero cape

...hidden somewhere.

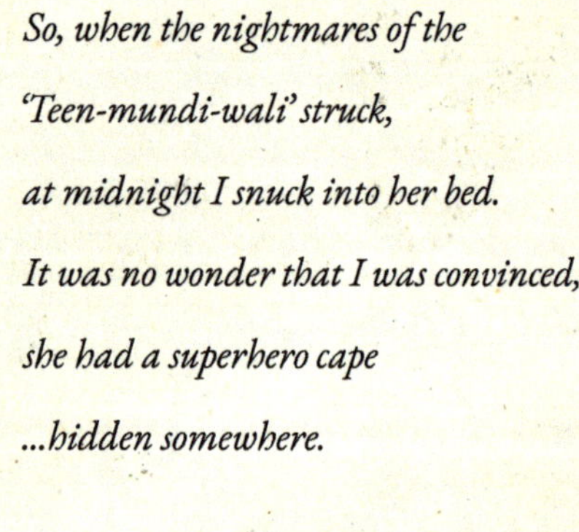

short term

It is a few moments before your eyelids tire, that you
reach out to the innards of your heart.

To think of you

Think of every goosebump that held on to your every
word, each glimpse, each look.
That fearless raw emotion that led me to hold on to the
idea that was you.
Led me to believe an idea was enough.
For me to tie all my happiness to.

As I fall asleep, I am aware when I wake up, I might
not remember this feeling.
The heavy heart will be calmer,
And these naked thoughts, will disappear.
And I realise...

Someday, you will too.

another day

A ripple then a wave.
You don't hesitate, don't behave.
Like the breezy autumns of Banglore,
you are what day-drinking is made for.

what to write?

What do I write about?

Sunlit days or crappy moods?

Nasty texts over comfort food?

Unkind words and a smile aloof?

What do I write? How do I amuse?

I could write about the hairy baboon,

who cartwheels on telly every noon.

I could write about the faint blue moon,

which was red last month, now due in June.

What do I write about? What do I have to prove?

Are we in a dance, did you just groove?

Or is this like a chess game renewed,

and did I just play my countermove?

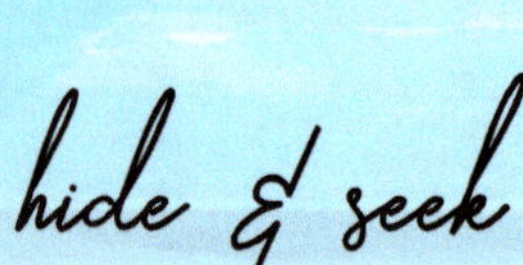

hide & seek

The memory lies hidden,
but nowhere has it gone.
Waiting behind the foolish grin,
and the world's aching song.
The day everybody is tired,
it will peep out to claim the game.
Splashing through puddles and waves,
shouting its lover's secret little name...

four legged pal

The world of fears ridden, of those smiles unbidden,
and a small little packet of pleasant sunny times,
Others won't hear, won't feel the pleasure sheer,
that I see in your eyes, and paws that slightly rise,
when I rub a little rub, behind your droopy hairy ear.

inside talk

"Hush, stay still," they said.

"Sure," I replied.

"But could you promise the same

to my fragmented dreams & what-could-have-beens

and all the leftover fantasies decorated

in my brain's hall of fame?"

treasure hunt

Somewhere on a map, must be an X marked.

Where lies buried a little casket, filled with

the bones of all my questionable past,

memories and wrong paths.

All for my pursuit of little happiness.

Memories and pictures will sting for a while.

But at the bottom is a wrinkled letter,

written only to remind,

why I chase new stories,

why I cross over bridges,

why I vowed to never regret.

For everything I did,

I did for an elusive feeling called happiness.

incase you didn't know...

We are all pretending here.

Pretending to care, pretending to be an expert,

pretending to be unmoved, pretending to be understood,

pretending to belong, pretending to be in love round the clock.

It is an exhausting charade we are used to.

Terrified of the uncertainty, we make planets to align and stars to cross,

and wear pretty porcelain masks with a smile, not letting a smirk out.

But we have that someone,

nudging through your cracks, not minding the grand mess inside,

with forceps of late-night chats and patient long walks,

filling the blanks, sponging off the stubborn face paint day and night.

Until pretending is only reserved for con calls, school plays and dating apps.

You either find that someone. Or be one.

The rest is all temporary.

dear old friend

Back then, when we shared a laugh,

you left with me a bit of you,

tied to an intimate memory,

before moving on to someone new.

Time stood still when immersed in a flashback,

I caught your view, in a profile online.

Felt a light breeze, heard a faint soundtrack,

And i realised, with you I left behind...

a precious bit of me, deeper than the skin,

buried under the act, hidden behind the wisecrack.

Perhaps the long-lost friendship, isn't all lost,

and the memory of that laugh, doesn't seem

that long back.

psst...

Sometimes people are only bearers,

of moments that fuel your insides.

The ones that stump, and you wonder,

where have you been all this while!

Those fables talk of soulmates,

isn't that too limiting to be real?

Can just one voice, one point of view,

hold a masterpiece like you dear?

Nope.

You need the caress of a village,

Or a scholar on acid to see you through.

And yet, if you do find happiness in a person,

Most probably that person is you.

something short

Maybe there is a sunny side to this lockdown,
we might turn into romantics again.
Deduce complex metaphors and devour thick books,
read between the lines, give hippie writers another look.
Scroll mindfully next time, pause at long poetries,
and maybe, just maybe...
not ask me to keep it short with dumbed-down word hooks.

the hug

If everything had gone right,

tomorrow, the 22nd day,

I would spot you across the street,

the harsh sunlight reflecting from your skin.

You would look around then notice me,

cross over to my side calmly,

then be a little reckless, a little desperate

with a frown that seems to suit your face.

A short trot and then pause a few feet away.

A hint of a smile, two steps more.

Then hug me tight, enough to suggest,

'not good with words, but hope this hug works,

to say I have been craving for this moment too.'

And I would have understood.

Only if everything had gone right.

kalopsia

Down deep into the Pinterest rabbit hole, one day I chanced upon a word.

Kalopsia - noun. a condition, state or delusion in which things appear more

beautiful than they really are.

The word was new, but the feeling felt familiar.

Throughout my tingling 20s. And then some towards my troubled 30s.

Sounded like the leftover of aching conversations,

the weightless freedom in a new friendship,

and the heady feeling of a trip long overdue.

But then, they called it a delusion.

Why not plain optimism?

Or the desperate need to day-dream?

Finding shapes in clouds, life lessons in songs,

and an obsession with happy endings?

An allure in random cracks

and urge to love a broken heart.

Or just be stubborn enough to find

a little speck of beauty,

in everything the world dismisses as painfully ugly.

inside out

The morning sun usually stayed at the windowsill,

but today, it bypassed the sheer curtains until,

it poured on my arm, like prancing crystal drops

to beckon me outdoors, to play, to show off.

But darling rays, even if I could get away

and sparkle like it was the '60s Bombay.

One step out, and I can no longer vouch,

that I won't attempt to get lost,

and fight against all odds,

to be unleashed inside out,

even if it offends the Gods.

the blue window

You hurriedly bid a small goodbye.

That summer noon, when the movers came,

they sealed the blue window, since that day.

And it changed colours every decade.

But do I smell a tiny hope? For this

morning, someone painted it blue again.

Is that a sign dear, are you near?

Is there a light on the other side?

Will I watch it open, perfectly framing my best bud?

Smiling against the blue window, every bit of the hippy weirdo,

set to reignite a friendship that was thicker than blood.

absence

If you are up there...

Would you know that when you left,

You stole away,

The little piece of heaven you had

That used to make my day?

piggy bank

Funny how bad decisions change shapes...

From fun to doubt and then grief,
until they hide in a piggy bank,
filled with other fine stories,
carefully marinated for an age,
when memories are all we will have.

mayhem

Even before I loved you,

I knew you came with a

kingdom worth of heartbreaks

and a spoonful of spice.

But you came all heart.

Misery, numbness,

and a soul about to fall apart.

One-part healer, two-part nuts,

like a middle-aged monk on psychedelic drugs.

You turn up the meter to devastate and then depart.

You were a messy, messy piece of art.

the last first

Not that I haven't
felt the euphoria of flying above the eagles,
or lost myself to the echoes of the ocean,
or discovered lonely pavements with a stranger on a calm night.

But moments end, and the earth keeps moving,
leaving behind a naked heart, longing to beat wildly like it did
the first time around.

sorrys

If sorrys could express,

yours would

be sleeping with the therapist.

lost wonder

Half a dozen tunnels opened to a sea of sunflowers.

While the sky turned grey for the moon to chase,

I invented a song to the rhythm of the train,

and hummed it the whole journey, and back again.

In an old movie scene, I spotted those sunflowers today,

and I remember my song, set to the beat of the rail.

Now all that is left,

is that naïve curiosity, the lost wonder,

and the little girl who recklessly stuck her head out

each time they opened the window pane.

not today

I don't have much to say

unlike most days.

Today I just want to curl up and dissipate,

spread inside pages, to live the lives of,

 charming murderers, misbehaved kids

and offensive women

 who refused to bite the bait.

not today

I don't have much to say

unlike most days.

Today I just want to curl up and dissipate,

spread inside pages, to live the lives of,

 charming murderers, misbehaved kids

and offensive women

 who refused to bite the bait.

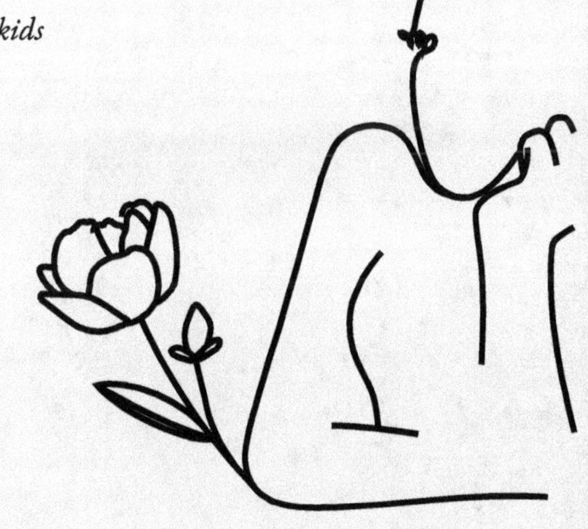

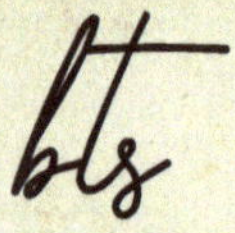

bts

Probably never right,

dazed and disillusioned,

off-centre, a hormonal mishap,

managed to find semblance

with someone completely unlike that.

Apologies if it looks easy.

But love performs more backflips than

a Russian acrobat.

We are a paradox, an anomaly.

Either a miracle, or just bad math.

We are not ending

in a bed of roses.

We are doomed for

a bloodbath.

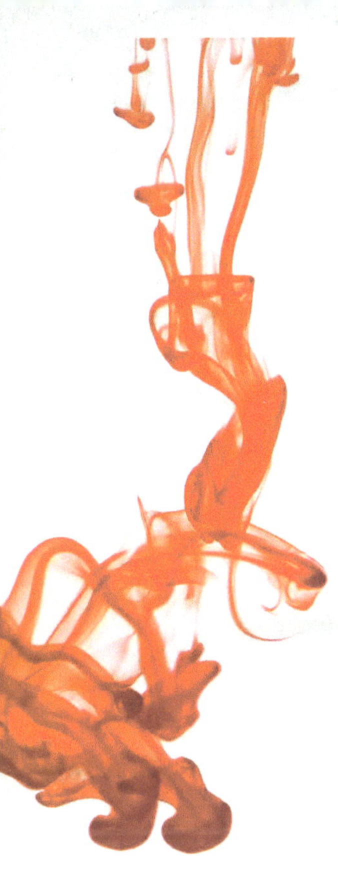

red ink

Remember your handwriting?

Was it squiggly like the veins on your legs,

or like an ECG pulse with a stray curve,

or are they filled with arcs and orbs,

like the torso of your damsel you observed?

And the last time you wrote...

did you surrender? Putting your pen to paper,

and wrote until the language fell short?

So raw, that you needed a break to soothe.

When was the last time you bled with ink,

when was the last time you wrote the truth?

puddle

The moon must know,
or maybe the daisies told him,
that they never looked prettier
than what they look like,
floating in a little puddle;

Even better than the company of stars,
or dancing merrily on a bed of fresh grass.
They looked beckoning in my lawn that night.
They looked like they could stay there together their whole lives

voice

I get it, you have tiny ripples in your mind

that turn to killer waves as it creeps into the night.

You are cooped up with thoughts familiar and strange

you like black and white, yet can't get rid of the greys.

In a world with no options, you talk out of choice

It gets better, but you can't ignore the noise,

How do I tell you, my love, I am on your side.

And if that wasn't enough.

I miss your voice!

legend

Half of the world made him a part of

their most clandestine stories,

through bits of a song, a dialogue, a wink, a smile.

He didn't care; he was deep in love with his art.

An affair that only led him to

be lodged deeper into the other half's hearts.

bland date

Conversations have been tedious of late

Faking skills on the verge of strain

In case I have missed any parlour tricks,

Bring them wrapped on the next date,

Faking can be the main course, boredom the dessert.

And you be the complimentary migraine.

no need

I could say I love you right now.

But what a waste it would be

of all the silences we had

that said much more,

effortlessly.

irrfan

'And yes, wait for me...'

...his voice fades out, ending the video announcing

his last movie.

I once waited in his study. For an hour

Little claustrophobic. A lot curious.

His gallery wall lined with books, garnished with trophies.

Books on politics, acting and Sahir Ludhianvi.

On the side was the National.Award. Like no big deal.

An air gun and two paintings on the floor,

in separate corners.

My eyes panned the room, taking it all in.

They halted at his figure,

standing at the door with a ponytail,

a huge smile and some

childlike excitement in his eyes.

People usually lie in magazine interviews.

I believed every word he said.

I didn't have to. I just did.

Why are those paintings on the ground?, I asked.

"They don't need my walls. They stand out wherever

they are kept." Just like himself.

I believed that too.

And a part of me will wait... eternally

'jo khatam ho kisi jagah, yeh aisa silsila nahi'   - Sahir Ludhianvi

www.ingramcontent.com/pod-product-compliance
Lightning Source LLC
Chambersburg PA
CBHW040946110726
48006CB00007B/1277